Animals that Fly

WITHDRAWN

By the water

great crested grebe

This bird lives mostly on lakes. It does not fly much. It dives to catch fish. The parents carry their chicks on their backs while they are small.

The kingfisher makes its nest in a bank by the water. It makes a tunnel with its beak and feet. The female lays her eggs at the end of the tunnel. This keeps the eggs safe.

mallard duck

Some ducks eat plants that grow in the water. They dive and pull bits off with their beaks. They also eat seeds.

stonechat

bluetit

reed warbler

moorhen

mute

great cr grebe

blackbird

All these birds live by the water. The kingfisher is a small bird. It uses its long beak to catch fish.

kestrel

rooks

lapwing

kingfisher

sand martins

heron

grey wagtail

This swan is cleaning its feathers. It scratches off mud with its beak. It picks out insects with its beak too.

This swan is going to land on the water. It spreads its wings out to slow down. It puts its feet out ready to land.

Swans can be dangerous. If they are afraid or angry they may hurt you.

rons are big birds.
ey often stand on one leg
a long time.
ey build their nests in trees.

3

Sea birds

The skua hunts penguins.

The pelican has a large pouch under its bill. It catches fish in its pouch.

Frigate birds steal food from other birds. They chase other birds until they drop the fish they have caught.

puffin

curlew

All these birds live by the sea. Some make their nests on cliffs. Others make their nests on the roc or on the sand.

4

cormorant

herring gull

oystercatcher

Herring gulls eat all kinds of food. In winter they look for bits of fish thrown away by fishermen.

The albatross is 3 metres long from the tip of one wing to the other. It follows fishing boats in case the men throw away any fish.

curlew

black-tailed godwit

ringed plover

common sandpiper

sanderling

All these birds are called waders, because they wade in shallow water. They often feed along the seashore.

ey eat things they can find
ar the seashore.
ey may eat small fish, or worms.
me eat shellfish and crabs.

5

Owls

Owls can frighten other animals that may attack them. They spread out their wings and stare at the enemy.

milky eagle owl

The snowy owl has white feathers. It lives in cold countries.

eagle owl

This is an eagle owl. It is one of the biggest owls.

Here are three long-eared owls. The ears are really long feathers. Owls sleep in the daytime.

Night birds

Here are some other birds that hunt at night. In the day they hide.

nightjar

This bird is chasing a moth. It eats all kinds of insects. It catches them as it flies.

nightjar

In the day it rests on the ground. Its feathers are the same colours as the ground, so it is hard to find.

tawny frogmouth

ost owls hunt at night.
ey hunt for food.
ey eat mice and small birds.
ey eat insects and frogs.

Birds of prey

Birds of prey are birds that hunt other animals for food. Vultures are birds of prey. They eat dead animals.

kestrel

This bird eats mice and rats, and some insects. This helps farmers, because these animals and insects eat crops.

This eagle eats small snakes. Sometimes it is called a serpent eagle. Serpent is another word for a snake.

golden eagle

This eagle is very big.
It can fly very fast.
It builds its nest
high up on a mountain.

Falcons are birds of prey.
They fly very fast and catch other
birds in the air. They catch them with
their claws.

Sparrowhawks hunt small birds, like
finches. Baby sparrowhawks eat
two or three small birds a day.

These are some of the animals that
birds of prey hunt for.

...gles eat other birds and hares.
...is one has caught a hare.
...an you see the baby eagles?

Tropical birds

The toucan lives mostly in South America. It has a huge beak. It eats berries.

Royal Flycatcher

Bird of Paradise

carmine bee-eater

red-billed hornb

little green heron

scarlet ib

These birds live in Africa.
They live by the water.
Many of them have bright feathers.

paradise flycatcher

egrets

greater flamingo

cattle egrets

These birds are looking for food. They eat tiny insects that live on the skin of other animals.

regent bowerbird

Some birds build very pretty nests. They decorate the nest with coloured stones and leaves, or bright feathers.

The hummingbird sucks nectar from flowers and eats small insects. It beats its wings very fast, and it is the only bird that can fly backwards.

amingoes have very long legs.
ey live in big groups.
ey build their nests in the water.

Nests

razorbill

This bird lays its egg on a cliff edge. It does not make a nest.

long-tailed tailorbird

The tailorbird sews two leaves together for its nest.

great crested grebe

This bird builds its nest on water. It makes a pile of weeds to lay its eggs on.

Most birds build nests.
The nest keeps the eggs safe.
Here are some of the places
where birds make their nests.

d woodpecker

long-tailed tit

little owl

Some nests are hidden in trees to keep the eggs safe.

The mother bird sits on the eggs to keep them warm.

After about two weeks the young birds hatch out of the eggs.

jay

The baby birds stay in the nest for about three weeks. The parents bring them food. They eat insects.

irds use all kinds of things
make their nests.
ome use grass and feathers.
thers use sticks or sheep's wool.

13

Food

Seed-eaters

macaw

crossbill

bataleur eagle

cardinal

bullfinch

Insect-eaters

black paradise
flycatcher

montague's harrier

rock wren

swallow

treecreeper

swifts

golden eagle

lyrebird

Birds eat all kinds of food.
Some birds eat fish.
Some birds eat meat.
Others eat fruit, seeds or insects.

Fruit-eaters

toucan

cock-of-the-rock

desert eagle owl

woodpecker finch

shrike

Tool-users

heron

Fish-eaters

vulture

kingfisher

ome birds eat eggs or shellfish.
ney drop stones on to the shells.
en the shells break
d they can eat what is inside.

15

Danger

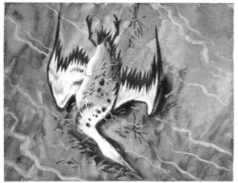

Many sea birds die because of oil in the sea. Ships throw away waste oil in the sea. The oil sticks to the birds' feathers and then they can't fly or swim.

Farmers spray their land with insect poison to stop insects eating the crops. Some birds eat the seeds and crops, and the poison kills them.

Some birds crash into wires because they do not see them. This can kill them. Others are hit by cars.

These men are making a new road.
They cut down trees and hedges.
Many birds have to find new homes.
Some of them die.

avocet

fox
cat
otter
hawk
pine marten

Some animals hunt birds to eat. Some eat birds' eggs. Here are some enemies of birds.

plover's eggs

Some birds hide their eggs on the ground. They are the same colour as the ground, so they are hard to see. Can you find the eggs in this picture?

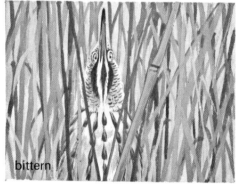

bittern

This bird is sitting on its nest. When it stretches up it looks like the reeds, so it is hard to find. This keeps it safe.

his bird is keeping its eggs safe.
covers the nest with its wings.
calls out to frighten
e other birds away.

Watching birds

You can watch birds in your garden. Put out food for them, especially in winter. Put out bread, fat and nuts.

Birds need water for drinking and bathing. You could make a bird bath in your garden.

You can watch birds build their nest. Try making a nest-box. Put it up in March, when most birds look for a place to build their nest.

This is a special park.
Many wild birds live here.
The birds are kept safe.
No-one can shoot them.

This man is putting a small ring round the bird's leg. The ring shows where the bird was found. If the bird is caught again later, people can see where it has come from.

This is called a hide. A man can hide inside. Birds cannot see him. He can photograph the birds through the hole.

This man has a tape recorder. He is recording the songs of birds that live in the grasses.

eople come and watch the birds.
hey can take photographs.
ome people draw the birds
r listen to their songs.

Keeping birds

Some people keep birds as pets. This boy is in a pet shop. He wants to buy a bird.

He gives his bird food and water every day. He puts the food in the cage.

The bird will sit on the boy's finger. It is tame. It can fly round the room.

zebra finch

java sparrow

orange-cheeked waxbill

budgerigar

finch

canary

lovebird

mynah

parakeet

parrot

All these birds can be kept as pets.
They live in cages.
Some have pretty songs.
Others can learn to say words.

Some people keep doves. The doves live in a dovecote.

Some rich people keep peacocks. A peacock's tail opens like a big fan.

You can see all kinds of water birds at the zoo or in parks.

Some people keep lots of birds. The birds live in a big cage in the garden.

Sport

Some people shoot birds. Here are some of the birds they can shoot. They are only allowed to shoot them for a few months each year.

These pigeons are going to race. The men will see which pigeon gets home first.

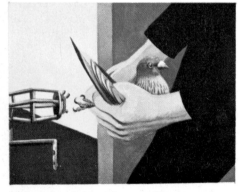

This is a racing pigeon. The man is putting a ring on its leg. The ring tells him who owns the pigeon.

mall

geese

These men are shooting wild birds. They hide in bushes so they can shoot ducks and geese.

canada geese

decoys

Long ago men trained cocks to fight each other. Men liked to watch and guess which cock would win.

Long ago men trained falcons to hunt other birds and small animals. Only rich people had falcons for hunting.

Hunting falcons wore hoods. The hood hid their eyes so they could not fly away. The hood was taken off when they were sent to hunt.

When they hit a bird
their dog runs to find it.
he dog brings the bird
ack to his master.

Bats

This is an old story about bats.
One day a weasel caught a bat.
The bat pretended it was a bird so
the weasel let it go.

Then the weasel caught the bat
again. This time the bat pretended to
be a mouse. So the weasel let it go
again.

This is a pattern on an old cloak
from China. Chinese people used
pictures of bats to mean long life.
Can you see the bats?

Most bats live in big groups.
In winter they sleep
in big caves.
They hang upside down to sleep.

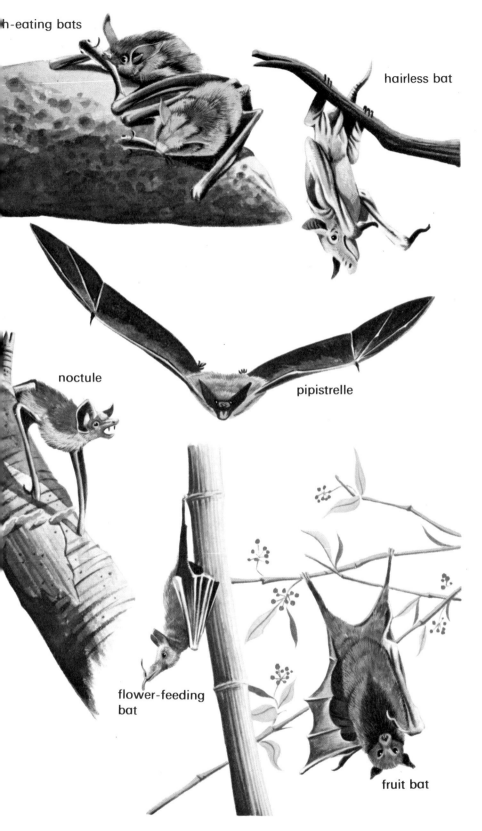

h-eating bats

hairless bat

noctule

pipistrelle

flower-feeding bat

fruit bat

This bat is called a flying fox.

Baby bats cannot fly at first. So their mother carries them like this.

Once soldiers made a plan to use bats in a war. They wanted to fix tiny bombs to the bats. The bats would carry the bombs into towns. No-one knows if the soldiers used their plan.

ats eat all kinds of things.
ome bats eat fruit.
ther bats eat fish.
an you find the bat that has no hair?

25

Other animals

flying phalanger

gliding frog

flying fish

All these animals
are called flying animals.

g squirrel

flying snake

go

flying lizard

ney can't really fly like birds.
ut they can jump
nd glide.

Finding a mate

great crested grebe

sage grouse

albatross

frigate bird

spotted bowerbird

mandarin duck

These birds are looking for a mate.
Some dance together.
Some show off their feathers.
One bird makes a pretty nest.

28